CHAMPIONSHIP
YO-YO
TRICKS

CHAMPIONSHIP YO-YO TRICKS

DAVE OLIVER

ILLUSTRATIONS BY JANE SMITH

METRO BOOKS

NEW YORK

© 2009 by Haldane Mason Ltd

This 2009 edition published by Metro Books,
by arrangement with Haldane Mason Ltd

A HALDANE MASON BOOK
Art Director: Ron Samuel
Illustrations: Jane Smith
The picture on page 5 is reproduced from a French fashion journal of 1791.

Metro Books
122 Fifth Avenue
New York NY 10011

ISBN: 978-1-4351-1935-6

Printed and bound in China

1 3 5 7 9 10 8 6 4 2

CONTENTS

YO-YO HISTORY

THE TOY THAT KEEPS COMING BACK!

The yo-yo seems like such a deceptively simple idea that it could have been around for centuries. In fact it has, sort of. There are reports of Filipino islanders using a sort of yo-yo to hunt animals—they hid in trees and threw it down at their prey, using the string to pull it back up again in case they missed. But those yo-yos were made of heavy stone, and not much good for doing tricks.

The modern yo-yo is still pretty old, and dates from 18th-century France. These first yo-yos were made from two discs of wood, joined at the middle, and attached to a string. You could bob them up and down, but not much else.

The breakthrough came in the 1920s, when American businessman Donald F. Duncan saw a slip-string yo-yo for the first time—the kind of string that allows the yo-yo to spin at the end—which had been imported from the Philippines. He realized its potential and began manufacturing this new type of yo-yo.

Now, all sorts of new tricks became possible, and the yo-yo craze swept across the US and later the world.

Mr Duncan also had the bright idea of teaching people to do yo-yo tricks—his yo-yo experts would travel around the country, demonstrating amazing tricks, and people would queue up to buy them.

Yo-yo crazes come and go, almost every new generation of kids seems to discover the possibilities, and new tricks are being invented all the time. Who knows? Maybe you'll come up with a few of your own, and the history of yo-yo will go on and on.

The modern yo-yo is based on something called a "bandalore" which was popular in France over 200 years ago. The woman playing with this yo-yo is from 1791.

YO-YO KNOW-HOW

MAKING A SLIP-KNOT

THE LOOP AT THE END OF THE STRING IS PROBABLY TOO BIG FOR YOUR FINGER, SO . . .

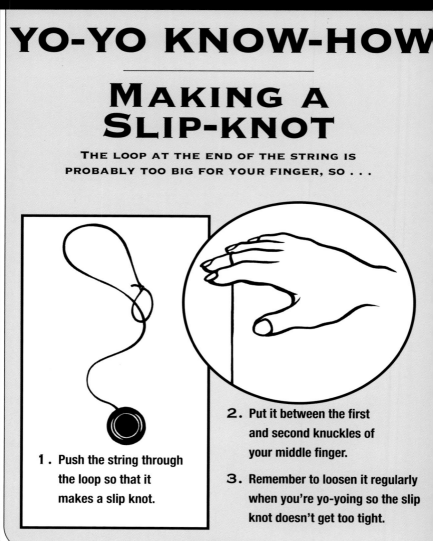

1. Push the string through the loop so that it makes a slip knot.

2. Put it between the first and second knuckles of your middle finger.

3. Remember to loosen it regularly when you're yo-yoing so the slip knot doesn't get too tight.

STRING LENGTH

CHECK THAT THE STRING IS THE RIGHT LENGTH FOR YOU

1. Hold your arm out straight in front of you and drop the yo-yo (with the string looped round your finger, of course).

2. When the yo-yo is at the end of the string, it should be between your knee and your ankle.

3. If the string is too long, you can cut it with scissors. Remember to leave a couple of inches to tie another loop. And if the string's too short, you're either too tall ... or you'll need another string.

4. Some people prefer it a little shorter (nearer your knee) or a little longer (nearer your ankle)—see which works best for you.

STRING TENSION

IF THE LOOP AROUND THE AXLE OF THE YO-YO IS TOO TIGHT, IT WON'T SPIN PROPERLY

1. Let the yo-yo dangle at the end of the string. If it spins clockwise, the string is too loose, if it spins anti-clockwise, it's too tight.

2. When the yo-yo stops spinning, the tension should be about right.

3. Spinning a yo-yo always changes the tension of the string—you'll need to do this every now and again to keep it right.

WINDING YOUR YO-YO

YO-YOS WORK BETTER WHEN YOU WIND THEM UP CORRECTLY

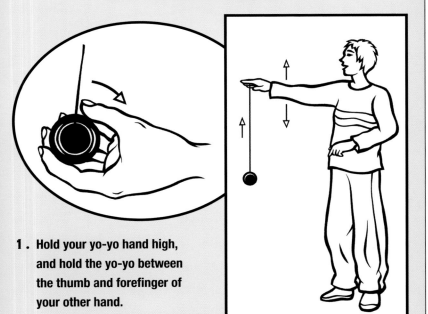

1. Hold your yo-yo hand high, and hold the yo-yo between the thumb and forefinger of your other hand.

2. Push down sharply with your thumb so that the yo-yo spins a little way up the string.

3. Move your yo-yo hand up and down until the yo-yo climbs all the way up the string to your hand.

THE THROW

IT'S ALL ABOUT THE TIMING . . .

1. Hold the yo-yo in your hand, palm upward, with the string running over the top of the yo-yo to your middle finger.

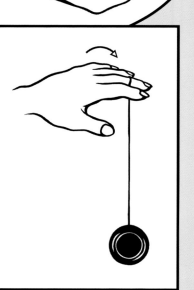

2. Throw the back of your hand down so that the yo-yo rolls over your middle finger and turn your hand round so it's palm down.

3. Just before the yo-yo reaches the bottom of the string, gently lift your hand upward.

4. If the yo-yo doesn't come all the way back to your hand, drop your hand a little, then raise it again as the yo-yo goes back down. With a little practice, it should come up higher each time until it reaches your hand.

5. Now you're ready for some tricks—turn the page . . .

13

EASY TRICKS

THE SPINNER

THIS IS THE BASIS FOR LOTS OF OTHER YO-YO TRICKS

1. Throw the yo-yo down in the normal way, but keep your hand still.

2. The yo-yo should spin at the end of the string.

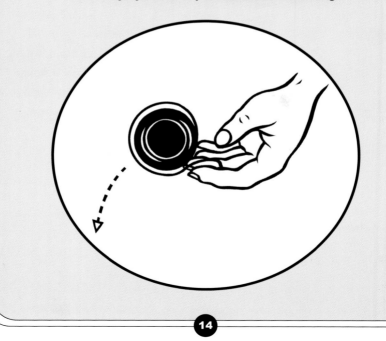

3. Jerk your hand up sharply to bring the yo-yo back.

4. If the yo-yo doesn't spin, check your string tension (see page 10), and make sure you're not lifting your hand up as the yo-yo reaches the end of the string.

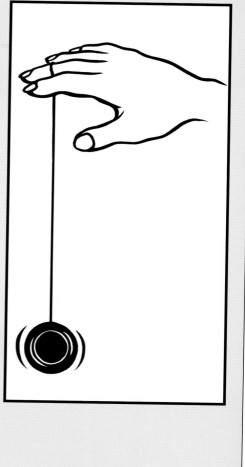

TIP

The faster you throw, the longer the yo-yo will spin. The longer it spins, the more advanced tricks you can do with it.

HOP THE FENCE

YOU GOTTA GET OVER IT!

1. Throw the yo-yo down.

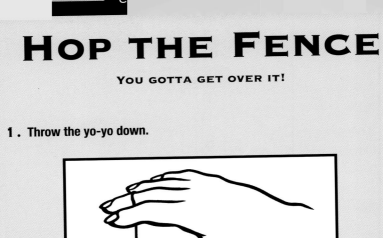

2. As the yo-yo comes back up the string, don't catch it, but flick it over your middle finger as it comes up.

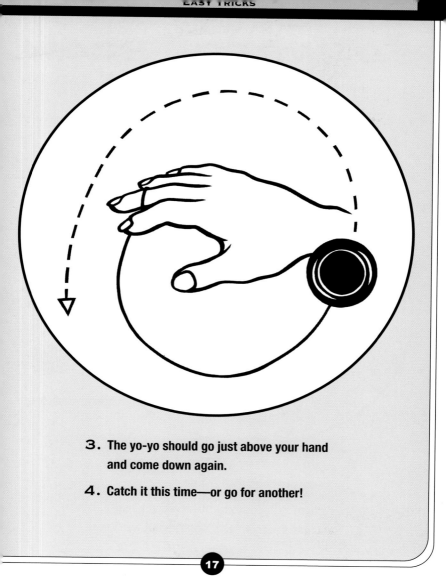

3. The yo-yo should go just above your hand and come down again.

4. Catch it this time—or go for another!

FORWARD THROW

GET OUT OF THE WAY!

1. Make sure you clear some space in front of you—at least as long as your yo-yo string.

2. Throw the yo-yo straight out in front of you.

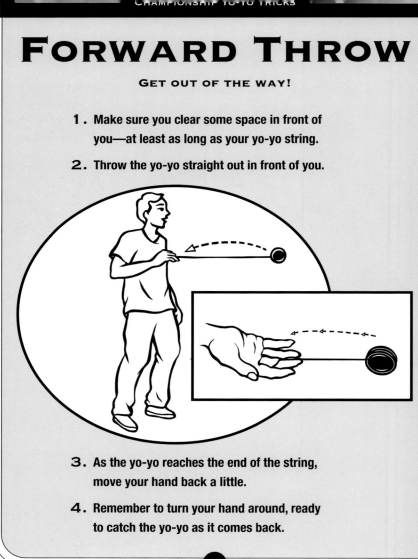

3. As the yo-yo reaches the end of the string, move your hand back a little.

4. Remember to turn your hand around, ready to catch the yo-yo as it comes back.

AROUND THE WORLD

THIS ONE TAKES A LOT OF SPACE AND LOOKS HARDER THAN IT REALLY IS

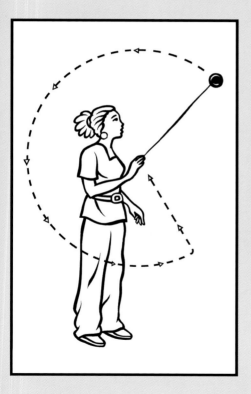

1. Do a Forward Throw (opposite), but aim it slightly upward.

2. As the yo-yo gets to the end of the string, move your finger around to the side.

3. The yo-yo should do a full circle around you.

4. When the yo-yo comes back in front of you, snap it back with a flick of your wrist.

LOOP THE LOOP

ROUND AND AROUND AND AROUND . . .

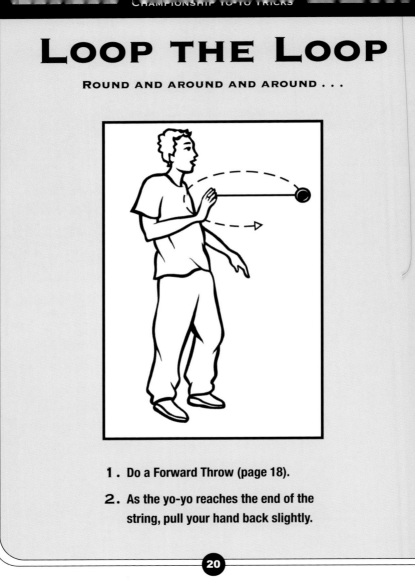

1. Do a Forward Throw (page 18).

2. As the yo-yo reaches the end of the string, pull your hand back slightly.

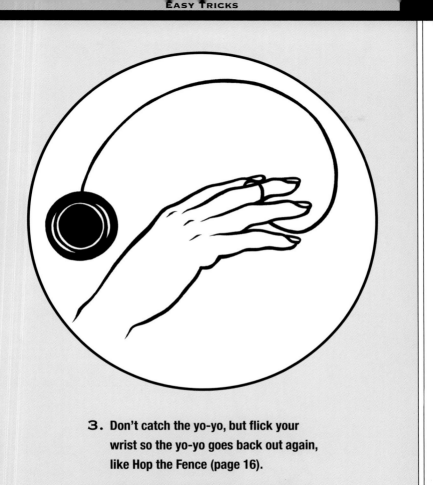

3. Don't catch the yo-yo, but flick your
   wrist so the yo-yo goes back out again,
   like Hop the Fence (page 16).

4. With a little practice, you can do this
   as many times as you like.

WALK THE DOG

THE PERFECT PET

1. Throw a Spinner (page 14).

2. Gently lower the yo-yo on to the floor.

3. Walk along next to the yo-yo as it "walks" along the floor.

4. Snap your wrist to bring the yo-yo back. Don't forget to say, "Here, boy!"

TIP

Touch the yo-yo to the floor gently, or it might bounce straight back up.

ROBIN HOOD

THE SHERIFF WON'T STAND A CHANCE
IF YOU GET THIS ONE RIGHT

1. Throw a Spinner
   (page 14).

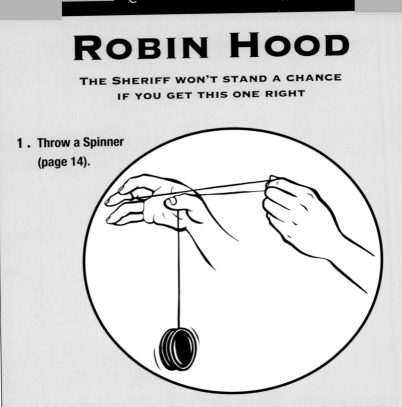

2. Drop your thumb down and put it against the string. Hook the finger of your left hand around the top of the string and draw it across your thumb, like pulling back an arrow in a bow.

3. When the yo-yo is a just below your hand, fire the arrow (let go of the string).

4. The yo-yo will drop and then snap back to your hand.

IN THE ELEVATOR

GOING UP!

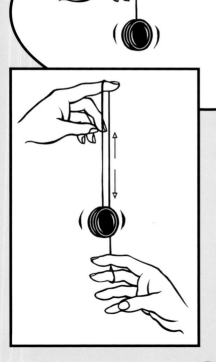

1. Throw a fast Spinner (page 14).

2. Draw the yo-yo upward over the finger of your other hand.

3. Take the string back down and thread it gently between the spinning yo-yo discs. Pull it gently down to draw the yo-yo elevator upward again.

4. When the elevator reaches the top floor, flip it over the roof and snap it back to your hand.

PINWHEEL

THIS SIMPLE LITTLE TRICK
ALWAYS LOOKS IMPRESSIVE

1. Throw a Spinner (page 14).

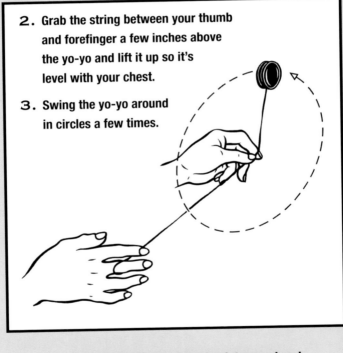

2. Grab the string between your thumb and forefinger a few inches above the yo-yo and lift it up so it's level with your chest.

3. Swing the yo-yo around in circles a few times.

4. Let go and jerk the yo-yo back to your hand.

THE CREEPER

THIS ONE LOOKS EVEN BETTER
IF YOU LIE ON THE FLOOR

1. Throw a Spinner (page 14).

2. Lower the yo-yo gently to the ground.

3. Lower your hand as it "creeps" along the floor.

4. When the string is fully outstretched, the yo-yo will snap back along the floor to your hand.

HARDER TRICKS

BAD DOG

SOMETIMES, YO-YOS JUST WON'T BEHAVE!

1. Throw the yo-yo down and behind you so that it goes between your legs.

2. As it starts to come back up the string, flick it up slightly.

3. If you do it right, the yo-yo should catch on your pants and "bite" them.

4. The yo-yo will stop spinning —rewind it (page 11).

TIP

Baggy pants made of thin material work best for this trick.

BREAKAWAY

THIS TRICK WORKS BEST IF YOU DO IT WITH A FLOURISH!

1. Throw the yo-yo in a Spinner (page 14) out and to your side.

2. As it reaches the end of the string, swing it slightly down and to the opposite side.

3. The yo-yo will spin on the end of the string and do a half circle.

4. Pull it back when it reaches the half circle point.

TIP

It looks really impressive if you don't look at the yo-yo, but keep eye contact with your audience throughout this trick.

ORBIT

AROUND THE WORLD AND THEN SOME

1. Throw a Breakaway (page 29) out to your side.

2. As the yo-yo reaches the end of the string, spin it up and around in a circle.

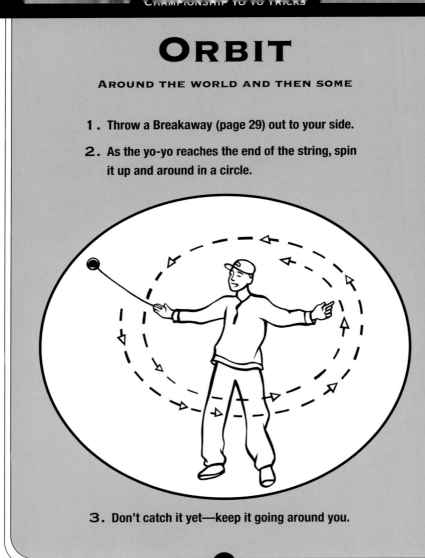

3. Don't catch it yet—keep it going around you.

4. Let the yo-yo do one and a half circles before you pull it back to your hand.

AROUND AGAIN

ONE GREAT TRICK + ANOTHER GREAT TRICK = AWESOME TRICK

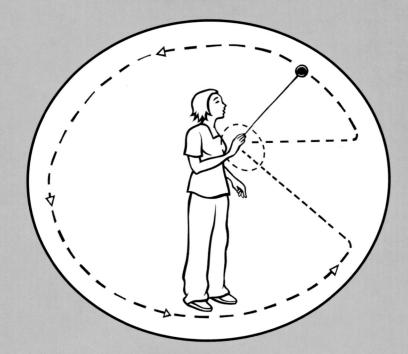

1. Do a Forward Throw (page 18).

2. As the yo-yo reaches the end of the string, flick it upward so it goes into an Around the World (page 19).

3. As the yo-yo returns to your hand, flick it around your hand and out again, like in Hop the Fence (page 16), so that it goes into another Around the World.

4. You can do this lots of times.

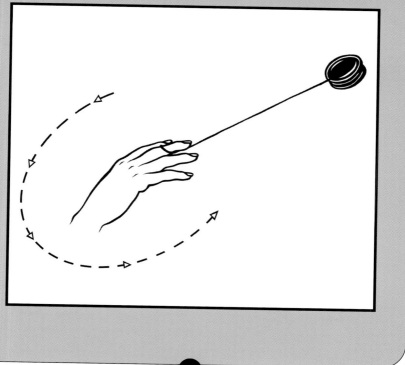

SHAMROCK

**YOU DON'T NEED THE LUCK OF THE IRISH
FOR THIS ONE, JUST LOTS OF PRACTICE**

1. Throw the yo-yo
out and up in a
high Forward
Throw (page 18).

2. When it comes back, flick it around your wrist and out again into a straight Forward Throw.

3. Next time it comes back, flick it around your wrist and down into a normal yo-yo throw.

4. Catch the yo-yo, accept applause.

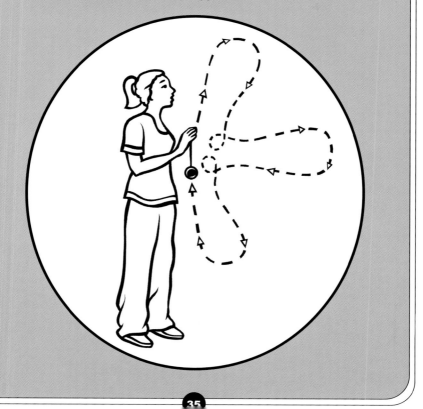

AROUND THE CORNER

THEY WON'T SEE THIS ONE COMING

1. Throw a Spinner (page 14).

2. Lift your hand up and round so that the yo-yo string hangs down behind your arm. Carry on moving your arm back until the yo-yo hangs down behind your right shoulder.

3. Bring your right hand back down in front of your shoulder until you can reach the string. Hold it a little above the yo-yo and swing it gently.

4. Finish by jerking the string and yo-yo sharply upward and let go—the yo-yo should fly up and over your shoulder and back to your hand.

SKY ROCKET

REACH FOR THE SKY!

1. Throw a Spinner (page 14).

2. Take the string loop off your finger and jerk the yo-yo upward.

3. As the yo-yo approaches your hand, let go of the string.

4. The yo-yo should fly skywards—
be ready to catch it when it falls.

TIP

For a really impressive finish, you can catch it in your shirt pocket.

SHOOT THE MOON

BE CAREFUL WITH THIS ONE, IT CAN GET DANGEROUS . . .

1. Throw a high Forward Throw (page 18).

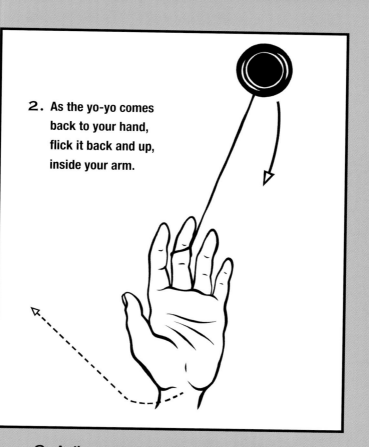

2. As the yo-yo comes back to your hand, flick it back and up, inside your arm.

3. As the yo-yo returns, flick it forward and up.

4. You can do this as many times as you like.

ROCK THE BABY

THIS IS A VERY NEAT TRICK WHICH TAKES SOME PRACTICE TO GET RIGHT. BUT WHEN YOU DO, IT'S WICKED.

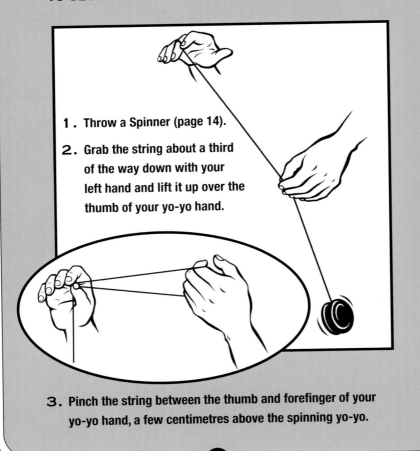

1. Throw a Spinner (page 14).

2. Grab the string about a third of the way down with your left hand and lift it up over the thumb of your yo-yo hand.

3. Pinch the string between the thumb and forefinger of your yo-yo hand, a few centimetres above the spinning yo-yo.

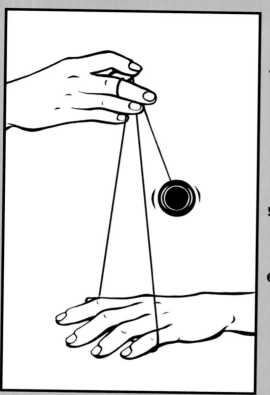

4. Move your left hand down and stretch your fingers out so that the string forms a triangle (this is the baby's crib).

5. Rock the baby back and forth a few times.

6. To finish, simply let go of the string. The yo-yo should drop and snap back to your hand.

TIP

Practice this trick with a "dead" yo-yo (one that's not spinning) until you get it right.

TIGHTROPE

YOU'LL NEED STEADY NERVES FOR THIS ONE

1. Throw the yo-yo out and to the side, like the start of Orbit (page 30).

2. As it comes round, put the forefinger of your other hand on the string a few inches above the yo-yo.

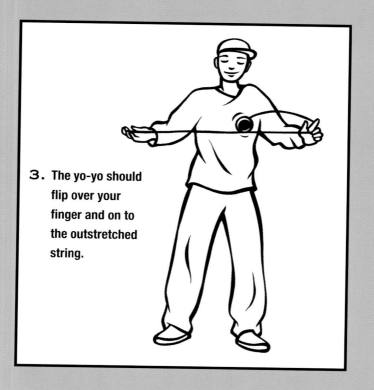

3. The yo-yo should flip over your finger and on to the outstretched string.

4. Let it walk the tightrope for a few seconds.

5. Flip the yo-yo off the string before it returns to your hand.

FLYING SAUCER

THEY COME IN PEACE

1. Throw a fast
Spinner (page 14)
down, but out and
away from you.

2. The yo-yo should
flip on to its side
and spin flat.

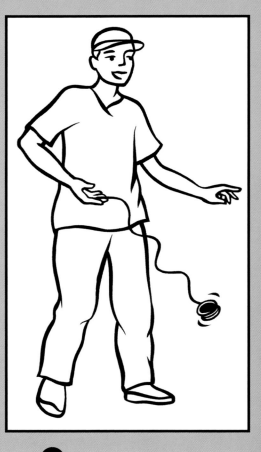

3. Hook the string over your thumb to make the flying saucer hover.

4. Jerk the yo-yo back to your hand.

GO FETCH!

PUT THAT DOG TO WORK

1. Throw a Spinner (page 14) and
   slip the string off your finger.

2. Drop the yo-yo gently
   on to the ground and
   watch it go!

3. Don't forget to shout, "Go fetch!"

ROUNDER

THERE ARE SO MANY TRICKS THAT START WITH A SPINNER (PAGE 14)

1. Throw a Spinner behind you.

2. Lower the yo-yo to the ground and drop down on one knee.

3. Let the yo-yo run around in a half circle before you snap it back to your hand.

UNION JACK

FLY THE FLAG

1. Throw a Spinner (page 14).

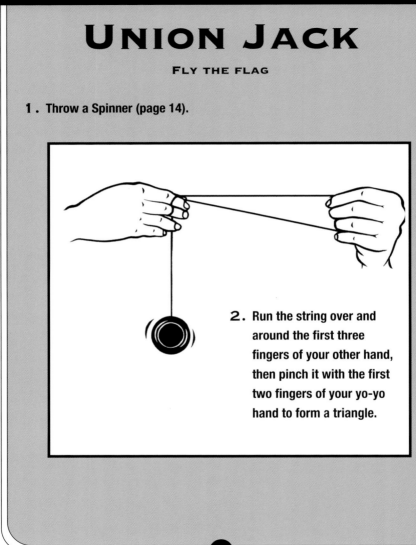

2. Run the string over and around the first three fingers of your other hand, then pinch it with the first two fingers of your yo-yo hand to form a triangle.

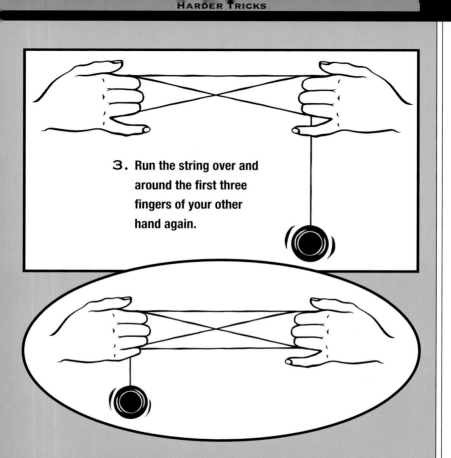

3. Run the string over and around the first three fingers of your other hand again.

4. Hook the string with the little finger on your yo-yo hand and pull it across to form the Union Jack.

5. Let go, and the yo-yo will return to your hand.

RATTLESNAKE

WATCH OUT—IT BITES!

1. Throw a Flying Saucer (page 46).

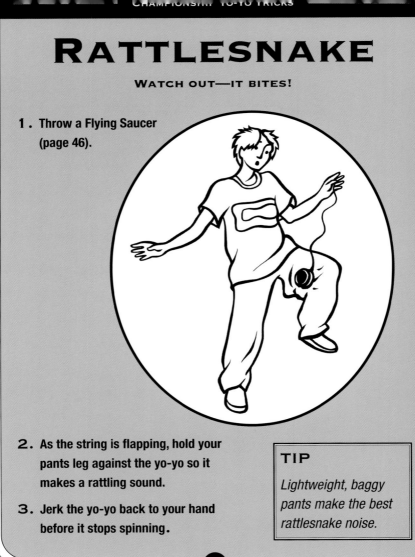

2. As the string is flapping, hold your pants leg against the yo-yo so it makes a rattling sound.

3. Jerk the yo-yo back to your hand before it stops spinning.

TIP

Lightweight, baggy pants make the best rattlesnake noise.

THROUGH THE HOOP

THAT DOG LOVES TO LEARN NEW TRICKS

1. Throw a Spinner (page 14) down behind you.

2. Touch the yo-yo to the ground and let it "walk" forwards through your legs.

3. Jerk the yo-yo back to return it to your hand.

MOTORBIKE

GET YOUR MOTOR RUNNIN'

1. Throw a fast Spinner (page 14).

2. Hook the forefinger of your other hand around the string a little over half way down.

3. Twist the string around itself and hook the thumb of your yo-yo hand through it to form a triangle. These are your handlebars.

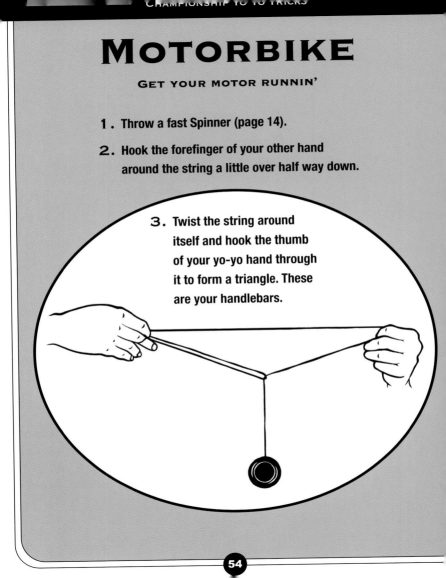

4. Touch the yo-yo to the floor and ride it like a mini motorbike.

TIP

Don't forget to do your best motorbike impression!

REALLY HARD TRICKS

DOUBLE OR NOTHING

TWO IS ALWAYS HARDER THAN ONE

1. Throw the yo-yo out and to the side.

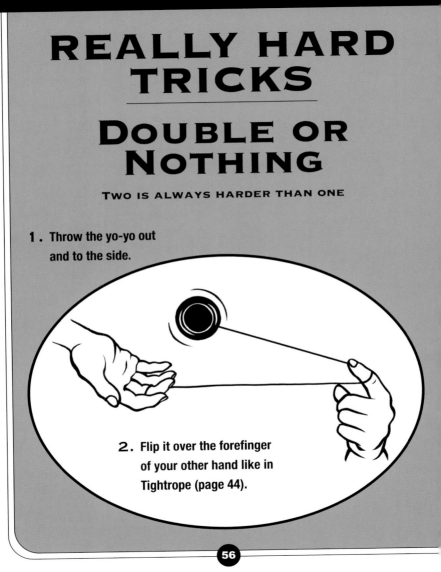

2. Flip it over the forefinger of your other hand like in Tightrope (page 44).

3. Stick out the forefinger of your yo-yo hand
   and let the yo-yo flip over that finger too.

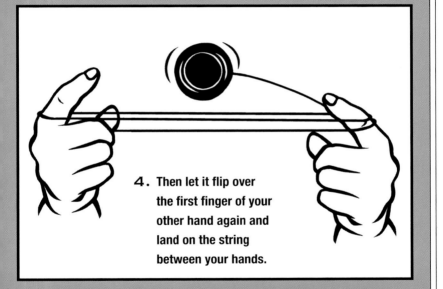

4. Then let it flip over
   the first finger of your
   other hand again and
   land on the string
   between your hands.

5. Slip your fingers out and let the yo-yo
   drop to bring it back to your hand.

UNDER THE FENCE

THIS WILL TAKE ALL YOUR CONCENTRATION AND DEXTERITY

1. Do a Forward Throw (page 18).

2. Swing it over and back like the start of Around the World (page 19), but directly behind you so it swings through your legs.

3. Flip the yo-yo over your finger as it comes between your legs and land it on the string.

4. Flick the yo-yo up to bring it back to your hand.

DROP IN THE BUCKET

THIS SPECTACULAR TRICK WILL PROVE YOU'RE A YO-YO CHAMPION!

1. Throw a fast Spinner (page 14).

2. Wrap the string around the thumb of your other hand and hold it between your first and second fingers.

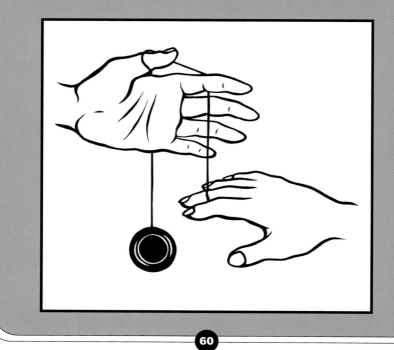

3. With your yo-yo hand, pull the lower string over your hand to make the bucket. This will pull the yo-yo upward.

4. When the yo-yo is near your hand, flip it over so it lands on the middle string of the bucket.

5. Flip it up and pull back to return the yo-yo to your hand.

DOUBLE TROUBLE

IT'S EASY WHEN YOU KNOW HOW!
YOU NEED TWO YO-YOS FOR THIS TRICK

1. Throw a Loop the Loop (page 20) with your normal yo-yo hand.

2. Then use the second yo-yo to throw another Loop the Loop with your other hand.

3. Keep them going, one after the other.

THE FINISH

ALWAYS FINISH WITH A FLOURISH!

1. Hold your pants pocket open as wide as you can.

2. Throw a Spinner (page 12) between your legs.

3. Swing it back up and into your open pocket.

TIP

You can't do this trick in jeans; make sure you're wearing baggy pants with big pockets.

INDEX OF TRICKS